WORLD ECONOMY EXPLAINED

Money and Credit

Sean Connolly

FRANKLIN WATTS
LONDON•SYDNEY

An Appleseed Editions book

First published in 2010 by Franklin Watts
338 Euston Road, London NW1 3BH

Franklin Watts Australia
Hachette Children's Books
Level 17/207 Kent St, Sydney, NSW 2000

© 2010 Appleseed Editions

Created by Appleseed Editions Ltd,
Well House, Friars Hill, Guestling,
East Sussex TN35 4ET

Designed by Helen James
Edited by Mary-Jane Wilkins
Picture research by Su Alexander

ISBN 978 1 4451 0045 6

Dewey Classification: 332.4

A CIP catalogue for this book is available from the British Library.

Photograph acknowledgements
Page 7 Tony Vilches/Alamy; 9 Basque Country-Mark Baynes/Alamy; 10 Alfredo Dagli
Orti/British Museum/The Art Archive; 12 Photos 12/Alamy; 14 A ROOM WITH
VIEWS/Alamy; 15 Schenectady Museum; Hall of Electrical History Foundation/Corbis;
16 Carrie Villines/Alamy; 19 Jeff Greenberg/Alamy; 20 Mary Evans Picture Library/
Alamy; 21 Kamyar ADL/Alamy; 23 Matt Griggs/Alamy; 24 Trinity Mirror/Mirrorpix/
Alamy; 27 Barry Stow Architect; 29 Bettmann/Corbis; 31 Reuters/Corbis; 32 World
History Archive/Alamy; 34 YM Yik/epa/Corbis; 36 Catchlight Visual Services/Alamy;
39 Nick David/PFEG; 40 Courtesy Barclays Bank; 43 Bjoern Sigurdsoen/epa/Corbis:
Front cover imagebroker/Alamy

Printed in China

Franklin Watts is a division of Hachette Children's Books,
an Hachette UK company.
www.hachette.co.uk

Contents

Understanding money

People have been fascinated by money for as long as it has existed. Think of some of the sayings, songs and advice you've heard about money. 'Money makes the world go round.' 'Money, money, money – it's a rich man's world.' 'The love of money is the root of all evil.' 'Neither a borrower nor a lender be.' 'A fool and his money are soon parted.'

People have very different ideas about the value of money, and sometimes those differing attitudes sit side by side inside someone's head. A proverb that reflects how money can give a person influence over others goes: 'He who pays the piper calls the tune'. We can probably agree with that. Then again most of us would agree with the saying: 'Health is better than wealth'. Maybe we're not millionaires sailing around on huge yachts, but we're not suffering from a heart attack or other stress-related illnesses either.

Can't live with it…

The complicated nature of money makes it a necessary evil: as some people might say, 'You can't live with it, but you can't live without it.' That very complexity means that it is important that we all try to understand money. Individuals, families and even countries base some of their most important decisions on how they treat money. If there is one thing about money that everyone can agree on, it is that money cannot be ignored.

In the middle of 2007, the world witnessed a massive upheaval that had money at its core. The focus was on credit – how easy or hard it is to borrow money – and this triggered one of the biggest economic crises for 80 years. What quickly became known as the credit crunch was the result of people making poor money decisions during the years which led up to it. The effects of the crisis will influence people's ideas about money (and credit) for many years to come.

Decades can pass between crises as serious as the credit crunch. During those interim periods, money continues to occupy people's thoughts – influencing political decisions, affecting jobs, defining how much houses are worth. Young people know that money will loom large when they become adults.

This book examines the many aspects of money and aims to explain how it works as well as how people can lose sight of both its power and its limitations.

Prices are marked in euros in this Italian fruit market. Italy used a currency called lira until 2002, when it changed to euros.

Fair exchange

We use money to pay for goods –

objects such as food, houses, clothing and computer equipment. We also use it to buy services, such as entertainment, education and insurance. We have a huge choice of ways to pay, but every transaction involves money passing from one person (or company) to another. Whether we hand coins to a newsagent or type bank details on a website, an agreed amount of money changes hands.

People who lived in the earliest cultures many thousands of years ago would have found the idea of exchanging coins and notes for something they wanted baffling. Neither paper money nor coins have any obvious value. They only become valuable and useful when national governments say they are valuable, and if people in those countries agree on that value. But how did societies develop this method of buying and selling goods?

Barter and trading

People throughout history have always exchanged goods and services. Schoolchildren exchange trading cards, conkers and even bits of their lunch. Without knowing it, they are using the same system of exchange as some of the earliest human societies – a system called barter.

In early societies people traded goods (often food) with each other using a barter system. A fisherman might trade a trout for a large melon. The deal would be made on the spot, perhaps after some bargaining. Even in modern societies, people sometimes swap items such as books or furniture – even houses – without using money. By doing so, they are continuing an age-old tradition. But straightforward bartering has not always been easy, or even possible.

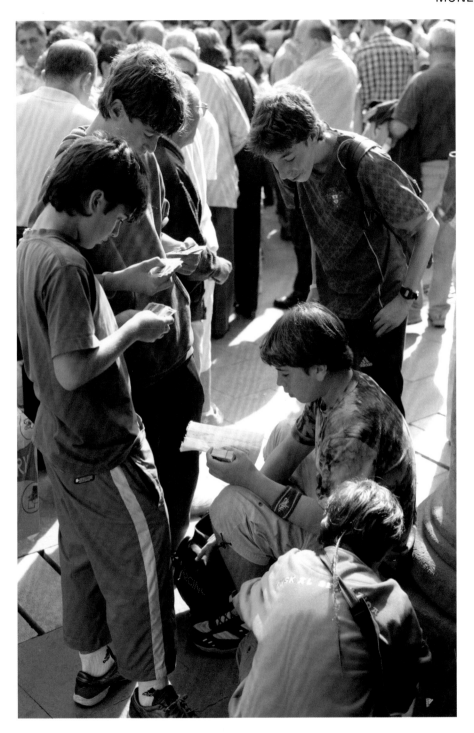

Spanish schoolboys swapping football cards. The urge to trade goods is basic and universal, with traders hoping to improve their position after a 'deal'.

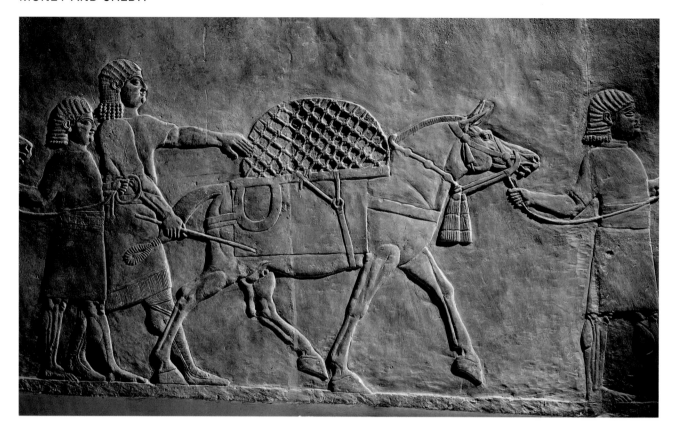

Even in simple societies which used barter systems, complications could arise. What happened if a fisherman wanted two melons from a farmer, but the farmer did not need two trout? If the farmer took two trout home, one might go off before he could eat it. People needed a way to store the value of the fish and the melons so that both could buy what they wanted when they wanted it.

Assyrian merchants transport goods on horseback. Middle Eastern peoples such as the Assyrians were using money more than 4000 years ago.

The solution for many cultures was to use valuable items, such as precious metals or shells, called commodities to store agreed amounts of value. The commodities had to be relatively scarce, which is why salt and gold were used rather than acorns or sand. Some societies may have used commodities as money as many as 100,000 years ago; archaeologists have found stone containers of precious dyes among valuable goods.

Developing a system

As primitive societies developed into more advanced civilizations, their system of paying also became more developed. The area around present-day Iraq is often called the cradle of civilization. The ancient Babylonians used barley as the basis for their commodity money and they created complex systems to use it which went far beyond simple exchanges between individuals. For example, by about 3000 BC people could use agreed amounts of barley to pay taxes and fines.

The first coins grew out of a similar tradition. Other civilizations in western Asia and Africa, including the ancient Egyptians, used valuable metals as forms of payment and exchange. In about 650 BC, the kingdom of Lydia (on the west coast of what is now Turkey) began forming metals into round pieces which were stamped with the image of the ruler. These were the first coins.

The Lydians traded a good deal with their neighbours, including the ancient Greeks, who soon adopted the system of using coins to buy and sell goods. This was the dawn of modern money, and the gold and silver coins of the eastern Mediterranean Sea became the examples for other countries to copy. Later governments, from the Romans onwards, built top secret coin-producing factories called mints which produced coins. Ordinary people often learned of a new king or queen because of the likeness they saw on new coins.

CLOSER EXAMINATION *CLOSER EXAMINATION* CLOSER EX

Clipping

Coins originally kept their value because they were supposed to contain a specific quantity of gold, silver or other valuable metal. The stamp on the coin guaranteed that. But people often clipped little bits off the edge of coins to collect some of the metals, and still tried to get the full value from the clipped coin.

Look after the pennies...

The coins we handle every day are part of a tradition that began almost three thousand years ago. A pound coin with an image of Queen Elizabeth II on it tells the holder about modern Britain, just as a coin carrying the image of Julius Caesar revealed details about ancient Rome. The image shows where the power resides within a nation – either symbolically in the case of the present queen, or in reality in the case of Caesar.

This Roman coin from the first century BC honours Julius Caesar. Caesar was the military leader who extended Rome's control to the North Sea with his conquests of ancient France and Britain.

If you were to flip the two coins described on the previous page, you would learn even more. The reverse of a Julius Caesar coin might show Romulus and Remus, the legendary founders of Rome, or Aeneas, a Trojan warrior who was said to have been the ancestor of the Romans. The reverse of a pound coin today might depict the royal seal or images relating to England, Wales, Scotland or Northern Ireland – the nations which make up today's United Kingdom.

National statements

These images have several purposes. On one level, they identify the places the coins come from. But on another level the traditional symbols add value to the coins. They act as a stamp of approval which tells people that the government produced the coins and can guarantee their worth.

That guarantee – or in some cases, promise – is important in the modern system of money. It also sets the modern system apart from those used until a few centuries ago. Most countries used commodity money – that is, coins containing amounts of precious metals – until the eighteenth or nineteenth centuries. Then as economies and populations grew, it became difficult for people to carry huge numbers of coins. In addition, producing the extra coins was expensive.

The next step was to use paper money (banknotes) as a form of representative money. In the past a coin had contained the metal that gave it value, but this new type of money was effectively a promise by the government to exchange the note for an agreed amount of a precious metal (usually gold).

Even that system became difficult to maintain, because banks or government treasury offices could not exchange large amounts of gold on demand. Governments then moved on to the type of money that nearly every country uses nowadays – fiat money. The word fiat comes from the Latin meaning 'let it be done'. Notes can no longer be redeemed for gold, but the fiat decree makes it clear that the government expects people to use the notes as legal payment for all transactions.

This system underpins all other methods of payment, including credit cards, cheques and online transactions. Confidence in any country's currency is ultimately linked to confidence in its government and other institutions. Which brings us back to the images of royal seals and national emblems on the coins and notes we use.

An amateur archaeologist uses a metal detector to search for ancient coins and treasure in the English countryside. Some finds are worth millions.

Personal account

HOLDING A PIECE OF HISTORY

Historians and economists can find documents and theories to explain how business was carried out in bygone ages, but some people prefer a more hands-on approach to studying the past. Coin-collecting is a hobby that gives people the chance to hold a piece of history in their hands. Dave Wood, a coin collector from Sussex, explains the attraction.

'What might this coin in your hand have bought two thousand years ago: was it used to buy bread, weapons, tools or for gambling? The answer is probably all of these things. Coins may not talk beyond their portraits and legends, but they certainly unlock the imagination and allow you to mingle amongst people from millennia gone by.'

EXAMINATION CLOSER EXAMINATION **CLOSER EXAMINATION** CLOSER EXAMINATION CLOSER

Telling a story

One of the most famous coins in history was struck by Brutus, one of the Romans who assassinated Julius Caesar in 44 BC. Brutus and his fellow conspirators called themselves the Liberators because they believed that Julius Caesar had assumed too much power. On 15 March (known to the Romans as the Ides of March) this group attacked Caesar with knives they had hidden in their clothing.

Brutus had coins made soon afterwards to mark the event. On one side of the coin was his own image. On the other side were the images of a cap (a Roman symbol of liberty) flanked by two daggers. Below was the inscription 'EID MAR' (Ides of March), a reminder that Rome's liberty was preserved on that date. The coins were used to pay Roman soldiers, reminding them that they were fighting for Roman liberty.

These two notes were printed by the Confederate States of America. This group of 11 states tried to become independent of the United States in 1861, but were defeated after a four-year civil war.

Credit where credit is due

Parents often explain finance by using examples from their children's experience. They might compare the family's decision to buy a car with their daughter's decision to buy a CD with her pocket money. Both purchases were made from a seller for an agreed price and the transactions took place with no argument on either side.

This piggybank is stuffed with dollars, the currency of the United States. This image reflects the traditional view that adults should save up for big purchases – such as houses, cars and furniture – by saving, just as children save their money in piggybanks. However, in the years leading up to the credit crunch, people were offered more and more credit to encourage them to make these purchases.

There is one big difference between those two transactions. The daughter knew exactly how much money she had, so she paid for her CD with cash from her purse. Her parents, however, were hardly likely to walk into a car showroom, decide on a model and start handing over thousands of pounds in cash. One way or another, they were likely to use credit to make the purchase.

Buy now, pay later

Credit is a form of delayed payment, a promise by the buyer to pay back a debt at a later date. Most people use credit to make large purchases, such as buying a house or a car, so they can spread the payments over a period of time. People also use credit when they do not carry a lot of cash. Even a very rich person would be unlikely to pay for a hotel room with cash.

The idea of using a promise to pay to complete a transaction goes back many years, almost as far back as money itself. European merchants used bills of exchange from Roman times to the Middle Ages to pay for goods when they reached foreign ports, rather than carrying large amounts of gold. A similar system used by Persian traders depended on slips of paper called *sakks*, which could be exchanged for money in countries as far away as China. Our word cheque also comes from that Persian word.

Cheques, like those early forms of payment, depend on the payer having enough money to cover the amount to be exchanged. Modern credit goes beyond that and involves a second transaction, which is 'buying' the money to pay for the first purchase. This purchase is called a loan and it must be paid back over an agreed period. Just as importantly, the person who needs the money (the borrower) must pay an extra amount, called interest. This is, in effect, the price of that second purchase (to get the payment money). Loans for houses are called mortgages.

Credit cards also use interest as a way of letting people 'buy' a bit more money. People receive monthly credit card statements listing all their purchases in the previous month. If they pay off the total amount, they pay no interest (and have been given up to a month to find money that they might not have had when they made some of the purchases). Any debt they carry over to the next month must be paid back with interest. Some people find it hard to control their credit card spending, which can lead to serious problems (see pages 20-25).

THE CREDIT-GO-ROUND

Sally (not her real name) is a single professional woman in her late twenties, who has had no formal financial training. However, she listens to the advice of friends who work in banks and other financial services.

'The first big thing I learned was that there's no real loyalty any more in this area. When I was growing up, I was led to believe that people opened a bank account and kept that same account active all their life.

'Maybe a person would get a credit card through the bank, and possibly a card with one of their favourite shops, but that would be it. If they ran up a big bill on a card, they'd be stuck with the problem of paying it off…

or face mounting interest. They wouldn't dream of going somewhere else for better credit.

'Then my banking friends started saying things like "How close is your relationship with your bank? Does it help you manage your debts, or does it simply use every chance to slap on extra charges?" That was a bit of an eye-opener, coming from people working in banks themselves. The same people urged me to take up advertised offers to transfer the balance of one credit card to another, to reduce the interest on what's due. I began doing that about two years ago and have even switched from one of the cards I switched to then.

'It gets a bit confusing, this credit-go-round, but sometimes I think it's the only way to stay ahead of the game. It's hard to resist the temptation to just spend, spend, spend because of some attractive deal. That money needs to be paid back sometime, interest or no interest.'

Web accounts

Like many other industries, banks have begun to use the Internet as a way of expanding their business. Customers can go online to find bank details that would otherwise involve making a visit to the branch, phoning them or writing a letter. Many banking transactions, such as transfers and withdrawals, can now be done online, at any time of the day or night. Some new banks exist only on the Internet.

Egg and First Direct are Internet banks that have no high street branches at all. In fact, they have no real branches or buildings. They claim to be able to offer customers better rates because their overheads are so low. Other banks have a larger number of staff and hundreds of branches to maintain. The online banks offer 24-hour convenience instead of bricks and mortar.

A sign announces 'Financing (credit) available' outside a group of new houses for sale in Florida in the US. The photo was taken during the boom years of easy borrowing before the credit crunch.

SINGLE FAMILY HOMES
FINANCING AVAILABLE
AVAILABLE LOTS 75 X 100
305-634-6070
www.Hiram-Homes.com

GRAND OPENING

YOUR MONEY'S WORTH

Pointing a finger

The credit crunch was a series of interconnected problems that affected the world economy in 2007. Can you think of any credit-related problems that might have caused or contributed to the credit crunch crisis?

Problems with money

Money has the power to make people's lives easier (and some believe happier), but that power can also be harmful. This combination of potent forces has given money the power to influence people's behaviour for better or worse. Most people believe their lives would be improved if they had more money. And many find it hard to deal with the problem of not having enough money.

A measure of worth

Most modern societies place a great deal of emphasis on the jobs people do to earn money. Some of this represents a genuine interest in what it is like to be, for example, a sports star or a writer. But much of the curiosity and respect is linked to people's earning power, or how

Above: a homeless man sells the Big Issue *magazine outside a shop in central London.*

much money they are paid in return for their work. When money becomes tight people feel under pressure. The shortage of money might come about simply because someone is careless with his or her money.

Mr Micawber, a character in Charles Dickens' novel *David Copperfield*, had this advice about money: 'Annual income twenty pounds, annual expenditure nineteen pounds nineteen and six [about £19.97], result happiness. Annual income twenty pounds, annual expenditure twenty pounds ought and six [£20.03], result misery.'

Opposite: entire families could end up in debtors' prisons if they could not pay their bills in Victorian England.

Mr Micawber was pointing out how fine a line there is between comfort and anxiety. In his view the balance can be maintained through careful housekeeping, but people may run low on money because of circumstances beyond their control, such as losing a job, becoming ill or because economic times are hard.

Bankruptcy

Sometimes people's debts mount up to the point where they cannot find a way to pay them back. This problem is as old as credit itself. Many countries use bankruptcy as a way of finding as fair a solution as possible between creditors (those who are owed money) and debtors (those who owe it).

People can choose to become bankrupt (this is known as filing for bankruptcy) or they can be forced into it by a creditor who is owed more than £750. Every country has its own rules on this. A bankrupt person must then cooperate with an official receiver, who examines the person's assets to see whether they can be sold to pay debts. Bankrupt people face many restrictions so that they do not run up more debt. They cannot use credit cards, become company directors or even have bank accounts. A period of bankruptcy lasts for a specific period (often a year) and after that the bankrupt person is discharged and allowed to resume activities that were banned during the bankruptcy. Although the official receiver might have come up with a three-year plan for the former bankrupt to continue paying some debts, all others are wiped out.

The idea of bankruptcy arose in England during the reign of Henry VIII, nearly 500 years ago. It came about as a way of protecting creditors and ensuring that they could force a debtor to pay back money that was owed. The modern version still tries to help creditors to recover their debts, but it also offers some relief for someone who owes money.

Political battles are constantly being fought about how much a government – or society in general – should help people when they face financial hardship. Some argue that the government has a responsibility to support a wide-ranging welfare state which helps people retain their self-esteem, so that they can be ready to work when things improve. Others argue that too many government handouts go to undeserving people, who would prefer to live on benefits than go out and look for work.

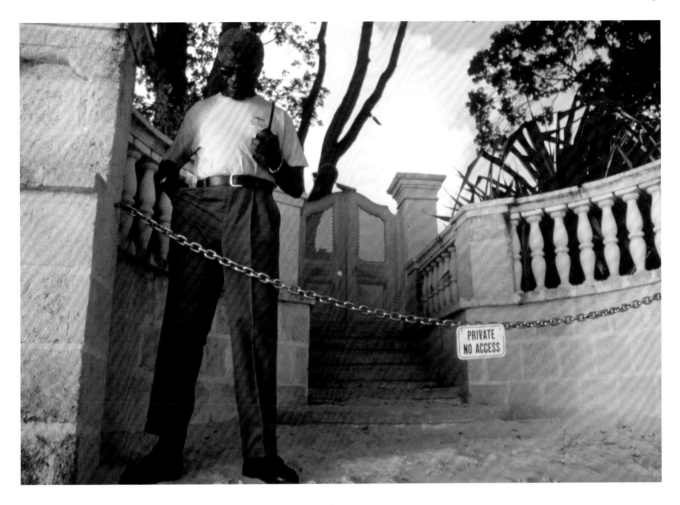

Too much money?

Perhaps it is hard to imagine having too much money, but many very well-off people (sometimes called the super-rich) have problems of their own, which less wealthy people might not even consider. One obvious problem is the constant threat of losing their money, for example, by being robbed. Thieves could be sizing up their expensive cars and boats, waiting to break into their luxurious houses, or plotting ways to cheat them out of their bank deposits. These fears may be coupled with anxiety about the risk of family members being kidnapped and their lives threatened unless a ransom is paid.

Enormous wealth may provide these people with possessions and financial security, but it also robs them of some freedom and adds extra layers of worry.

A security officer guards the gate leading to an upmarket beach on the Caribbean resort island of Barbados.

A healthy balance

Mr Micawber's thoughts about careful housekeeping on page 21 also apply to national economic policies. Most voters choose the political party they think will handle the nation's finances (or national income) best. They believe that all aspects of a nation's health and prosperity are affected by how carefully its government manages the country's finances.

Exactly where national income comes from is a matter of political debate within every country. Should the

British policemen battle with strikers during the coal miners' strike which threatened the national economy in 1972.

government raise taxes or cut costs? Even people who favour low taxes and few financial regulations agree that a national government has many financial responsibilities.

Forming policies

A national government can be compared with someone who runs a household and looks after the family budget. Schools and hospitals need to be built or repaired, just as families need to buy clothing and food. Education is a big concern for both – the government makes decisions about training and paying teachers while a family may need to buy computers and other equipment to help pupils through their school years.

All these decisions are affected by the budget – the precise amount of money coming in and going out. Families add money to their budgets through their income (money they earn) and their investments. Governments use the money raised by various taxes to pay for expenditure that they believe is necessary or unavoidable.

Just as individuals and families choose to borrow money for their largest purchases (for example, car loans and mortgages), governments also borrow money. Most governments do this by issuing government bonds, which are like loans. The bonds are usually for a set amount of the national currency. British bonds are in pounds sterling and Canadian or Australian bonds are in dollars.

The people who buy the bonds are actually lending the country the money they pay for the bonds. They expect a certain amount of interest to be paid on their investment, either at regular intervals or after a specific

YOUR MONEY'S WORTH

Costs and benefits?

Governments raise much of the money that they need to spend through taxes which people pay on the money they earn (their incomes). Tax is also paid by businesses, by customers buying alcohol or tobacco, by car-owners buying tax discs, on petrol and in other ways. The tax we pay is a constant source of disagreement between political parties.

Just as important is how that money is spent. Many countries, including Great Britain, have a system of universal benefits that are paid to families or individuals regardless of how wealthy they are. Some people argue that these payments are wasteful and that better-off people should not receive them. Others argue that means testing, the best way to find out how wealthy someone is, invades people's privacy. What do you think?

Inflation

Governments sometimes use money as a tool in a different way from simply collecting taxes and making payments. Central banks watch interest rates with an eye towards foreign trade (see pages 30-31) or even buy back bonds to 'kick start' the economy, and governments also have monetary policies with clear aims. These policies are designed to create a stable climate for businesses so that companies can thrive and produce wealth within a country and so families can manage their expenses without unexpected shocks.

One of the problems that monetary policy addresses is inflation, or the dramatic rise in prices over a long time. If prices in a country rise by, say, 15 per cent a year (this was Britain's inflation rate in 1978), then the national currency will lose value over the same period. If wages keep pace with price rises, some people argue that this should not be a problem. But uncertainty about future prices may stop people investing their money in that country. They may invest in other countries with steadier economies instead.

Most economists today believe that inflation can be caused by too much money in the economy. Economists often advise countries to reduce the national money supply as a first step in the battle against inflation. Governments can have an influence, but the central banks hold the real power and they look at what is happening abroad when making decisions.

length of time, when the bond is said to mature. Governments also borrow from banks in their own countries. People buy bonds and banks lend to governments because they are thought to be good risks. In other words, a government is unlikely to default on (not pay) a debt because it can usually find money to repay it by raising taxes. Some countries, however, have unstable governments which cannot sell bonds or find lenders within their own borders. These countries borrow from international institutions such as the World Bank and the International Monetary Fund (IMF).

The World Bank and IMF, along with regional institutions such as the Asian Development Bank and African Development Bank, focus on helping the poorest and least stable countries. Their aim is to help countries help themselves by using loans to build or rebuild their economies.

But those same institutions are often accused of playing politics by forcing countries which borrow money from them to accept strict conditions (controls) on how they spend the money. Those conditions often involve changing the way people in the country borrowing the money have done business for decades or even centuries. Changing those customs overnight can be disruptive, and many countries have suffered riots and even rebellions as a result.

The Ugandan government has used World Bank funds to investigate the possibility of creating a heritage trail in the south west. The trail would raise awareness of Uganda's rich history and attract tourists.

The global view

One famous saying about money:

'money makes the world go round' is the title of a song from the musical *Cabaret*. The words of the song tell us that every currency has the power to make the world change, whether it is the mark (Germany's currency before the euro), the Japanese yen, the American buck (slang for dollar) or British pound.

One verse from the song goes:
'A mark, a yen, a buck, or a pound
A buck or a pound
A buck or a pound
Is all that makes the world go around,
That clinking clanking sound
Can make the world go round.'

Cabaret is set in the German capital, Berlin, in 1931. The date is important for two reasons. One is that Adolf Hitler's Nazi party was beginning to become more influential in Germany by then, and there is a feeling of menace running through the musical. The second reason is that in 1931 Germany had experienced a crisis with its national currency, the mark. The reasons for this went back several years.

In 1923 Germany went through a time of political unrest when there were huge strikes that closed down many industries for long periods. The government (rather than companies) had to pay the millions of workers who then had no job, so it began printing more and more money. A sudden increase in money supply triggers inflation (see page 26) and prices across Germany began to rocket. Eventually the mark became almost worthless, so people had to take wheelbarrows full of banknotes to pay for a single loaf of bread or piece of meat.

Liza Minnelli and Joel Grey sing the duet 'Money Makes the World Go Round' in the film version of the musical Cabaret, *which is set in Germany between the two World Wars.*

The Germans solved this problem within about three years, but the hyperinflation they had suffered remained a painful memory. Hitler convinced many people that he would never allow Germany to be humiliated again.

Central control

The Germans are not the only people to have heeded the lesson of that brush with hyperinflation. Economists and government leaders around the world agree that it is vital to keep their national currencies stable. This stability, which means that a pound or dollar will still have value six months or ten years from now, helps to build confidence in both the currency and the country it represents.

That is where governments and other national structures can play a part. Most countries have central banks that affect the flow and availability of money – especially in banks and other financial institutions. The Bank of England, the Federal Reserve (America's central bank) and others use their power to raise and lower interest rates within their countries and to make some transactions easier (or more expensive).

The activity of a country's central bank has effects outside that country. For example, if the Bank of England raises interest rates, British banks usually follow their example. As a result the people who deposit money with these banks receive more interest on their investment. That applies to foreigners as well as British people. So if someone sells dollars to buy pounds to invest in a British bank, the pound becomes worth a bit more (because it is in demand)… and the dollar loses a little of its value against the pound.

Many other factors affect what are called exchange rates, and foreign exchange dealers (who work for banks or represent customers) play the market by trying to predict whether a particular currency is rising or falling in relation to other currencies.

Weak or strong

Things become even more complicated when currencies rise or fall sharply. British holidaymakers flocked to the US in 2007,

YOUR MONEY'S WORTH

Euro or no euro?

One of the fiercest political debates in Britain centres on the euro, and whether Britain should adopt it as a currency. Critics of the euro claim that Britain would suffer, losing jobs and exports while paying higher prices, if sterling were abandoned.

Euro supporters say that the euro would provide Britain with a stronger international currency and also send out a signal that Britain is part of a European team, resulting in Britain being given better terms in the European Union.

knowing that each of their pounds was worth more than two dollars. Exchange rates had changed dramatically by the end of 2008, when the pound was worth only about $1.48, down from a high of $2.12 about eighteen months earlier. At a result of the change in exchange rates, restaurant meals, hotels and car hire in the US had become more expensive. At the same time goods that Britain exported to the United States became cheaper because of the fall in value of the pound. This made them more attractive to American buyers and helped British companies.

Governments and central banks need to find a balance between these extremes, but they also know that rises or falls in currency values aren't all bad – or good.

Anti-euro protesters in Britain portray their cause as a patriotic defence of their country's right to manage its own affairs.

The credit crunch

Losing a job or being unable to pay

back a loan is a devastating problem for anyone to face. It might take years to return to a stable financial situation. This can happen to countries too. Germany's hyperinflation, which has recently been repeated in Zimbabwe, had a long-term effect on its outlook. These events may seem relatively insignificant when they affect just one country, but imagine the effect of worldwide economic upheaval.

Personal account

TAKING RISKS

For decades banks and bank officials had been famous for being careful handlers of other people's money. People felt that money invested in a bank would not only be protected by this careful handling, but that it would grow steadily. In short, banks offered customers a way of becoming a little bit wealthier, but not too fast and without having to take too many chances with their money.

By the 1990s, though, many banks had abandoned their cautious approach as they tried to speed up the process of creating wealth.

Lehman Brothers was an example. Under the control of its chief executive Richard (Dick) Fuld, the bank grew richer and richer. Its share price rose from $4 (about £2.50) in 1994 to $82 (£51) in 2007.

Larry McDonald, a Lehman vice-president during that period, explained how Lehmans grew so quickly – which is also why it collapsed so spectacularly: 'Dick Fuld essentially said to our head risk-taker in commercial mortgage-backed securities: "You've got to take more risk. Risk, risk, risk, risk, risk, and that risk leads to the bottom line (final profit)."'

Opposite: the Great Depression of the 1930s hit north east England especially hard. Unemployed miners and shipbuilders marched nearly 500 kilometres from Jarrow to London in October 1936 to protest against poverty.

The world has had several global economic crises. One was the Great Depression of the 1930s, when millions of people around the world lost their jobs, and in many cases, their homes. More recently, countries around the world have been hit by a series of events called the credit crunch, which began in 2007.

Boom and bust

The credit crunch came at the end of an apparently stable economic time, like the Great Depression of the 1930s. A period of optimism, when money is lent freely to set up businesses or to buy houses and when the value of people's investments climbs, is called a boom.

The problem with booms is that people expect them to last for ever, so they take risks and lose some of the caution that bankers usually use.

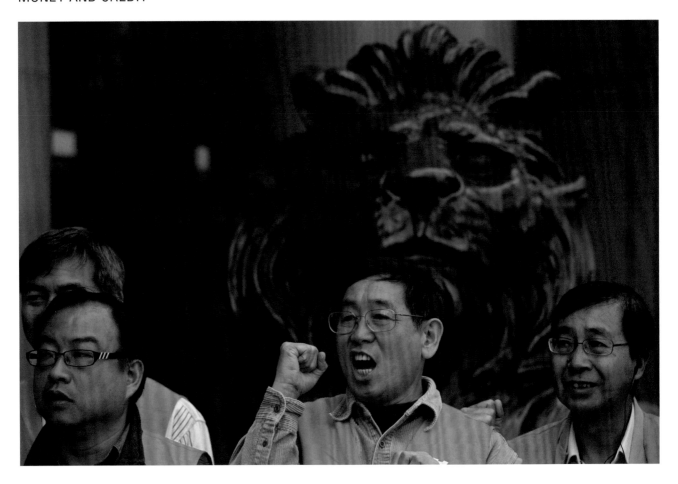

During the early 2000s house prices rose rapidly in many countries, especially the United States. American banks began lending money to customers who would not usually be offered mortgages because they might have difficulty repaying them. The banks believed that even if these borrowers defaulted (did not repay the loans), the banks could sell the properties to recover the borrowed money.

Then house prices began to fall in late 2006 and when people began to default on their mortgage loans, their houses could not be sold. Banks began to lose lots of money. Then it emerged that other (usually cautious) financial institutions had invested in the banks that were losing money, so they were also losing money. Twenty-first century banking is international, which meant that banks around the world had invested in the American banks and financial institutions that were at the heart of the problems.

Members of the Hong Kong Banking Employees Association stage a protest outside the headquarters of HSBC in February 2009. HSBC was preparing to get rid of 1000 of its 18,000 Hong Kong staff because of the credit crunch.

Putting more money in

As well as raising money through taxes, governments can raise cash by issuing bonds. Individuals and – to a much greater extent – banks buy these bonds, which are in effect promises by the government to pay back those buyers with additional interest at a later date. Bonds are considered to be safe investments, which is why they are attractive. But there is a side effect: a lot of banking assets are tied up in these promises, rather than in the form of cash which could be used to make loans to companies and individuals. Many economists believe that the best way to end a recession like the credit crunch is to get more money moving through the economy. If companies find it easier to take out loans they can develop and grow more quickly, creating more jobs and helping the country dig its way out of recession. In 2009 the Bank of England used just such a tactic, which it calls quantitative easing. By August 2009 it had pumped £175 billion into the British economy.

People around the world began to feel knock-on effects when the boom went bust. Banks were at risk and found it hard to pay back their depositors' money. Other banks almost stopped lending altogether, so it became almost impossible for companies to grow or for new ones to start up. Unemployment grew and with it grew a widespread resentment towards the bankers many people blamed for the crisis.

During the boom, many high-earning bankers had earned big bonuses by taking risks that led to quick profits. Now, with the crisis in full swing, these same bankers were seen as the culprits. For many observers, the credit crunch really became serious when Lehman Brothers, one of the oldest and most respected American banks, collapsed on 14 September 2008. If that bank went under, who else might follow?

Starting young

Young people have never been under as much pressure as they are today to learn about money. They need to learn how to make important decisions comparatively early in their lives. Even by the age of 12, some students have mobile phones and may need to choose the right payment plan.

Later, when college or university looms, they need to understand about student loans, interest rates, investment schemes and other aspects of the financial world.

Pupils can find advice on all these issues at school, or in local libraries, at a bank or on the Internet. Most adults welcome questions about how to handle financial affairs. Some young people even find that the places they might visit for advice, such as their local bank, can offer a career that might suit them in later life.

Inside school

Opposite: young people often start earning by babysitting or doing other locally based jobs. This work helps to prepare them for the important decisions about money they will need to make in later life.

Many government educational advisers would like some form of financial education to be included in the national curriculum, the official guidelines setting out what should be taught in schools. The reasons for, and the benefits from, such teaching are obvious. Even very young children are aware that their families have had to cope with the problems of the credit crunch (see pages 32-35). Having a basic grounding in the events that led to the crunch, and the effects it had, could help them make sensible decisions when they are older.

Even without the credit crunch, the financial world has been changing at an unprecedented rate. It is hard for adults to keep track of new methods of payment and a new wave of investment opportunities.

Personal account

FINANCIAL LITERACY

Graham Durgan is a member of Britain's Institute of Chartered Accountants. He is trying to help schools in England and Wales begin to teach what he calls financial literacy. But before they can do that he believes that young people need to become far more confident with numbers. 'We find there are some real problems with basic numeracy,' he has observed. 'Fifty per cent of school leavers don't understand what 50% means.'

Richard Branson: onward and upward

Richard Branson is one of the best recognized business leaders in the world. Successful, yet informal and down to earth, he has succeeded in many areas of business and has offered skills and advice to young people as well as contributing to government attempts to promote business skills. Branson's success is all the more impressive because he had to overcome dyslexia as a child.

Like many successful people in business, Branson started young. He began his first business, producing a young people's magazine called the *Student*, in 1966 when he was only 16. Four years later he set up the Virgin Record Company, sending out records by post. He then opened the first Virgin Records store on Oxford Street in London, and soon after that widened this music business by opening a recording studio. By 1972 Branson had attracted some big-name musicians to Virgin Records; a series of popular albums at that time added money to the Virgin bank account and Branson continued to broaden and improve the Virgin Company.

Over the next few decades, the Virgin brand name became a competitor in many areas of business, ranging from long-haul air travel through mobile phones to trains. In 1999, Branson was knighted for his services to British industry. Throughout his long business career, he has never lost the enthusiasm he had as a young man and he believes his success stems from the ability to maintain a youthful outlook.

Children today need to learn financial skills far earlier than their parents did. An 18-year-old starting university could earn a degree three years later but may also take out student loans which leave her £20,000 in debt.

Some people are concerned that students are leaving school without the skills to deal with their new responsibilities. Some of the problems are connected to a poor understanding of the basic applications of maths. If young people can gain confidence in mathematical skills, they will be better prepared to face the challenges of the wider world.

Translating those skills into practice is a challenge, but educational authorities are meeting that challenge in some interesting ways.

Since 2000, English schoolchildren have benefited from programmes linking their schools with outside organizations which specialize in financial education. One such organization is the charity Personal Finance Education Group (pfeg), which helps schools and teachers introduce young people to the world of money and finance. It aims to have its a wide-ranging programme of financial education (called What Money Means) available to all primary schools in England by 2011.

Gaining confidence with numbers is an essential part of learning how to manage money in later life. Primary school pupils can learn to make connections between maths lessons and applications in their daily lives.

Into the future

People often say that no one would have predicted some of the recent developments in communications and transport 50 or even 30 years ago. The same could be said about the ways in which money and credit are changing. No one predicted the impact of the Internet in 1960 or 1980, or that most people, including teenagers, would have their own mobile phones.

The Internet and mobile phone technology have played a big part in changing the world of money and credit. Computer users can go online to buy books, air travel, concert tickets and items on an auction site such as eBay.

This progress is not just centred on people living in the most well-off countries. Many people living in rural Africa and Asia have mobile phones which they can use to move money from one bank account to another, sometimes sending amounts to people in other countries.

Expect the unexpected

The most successful businesses – and business leaders – know that nothing remains the same and that if they expect the unexpected they will not be left behind. The same can be said of our understanding of money and, especially, of credit. At the most basic level, people will continue to earn, win, lose and spend dollars, pounds and euros. But it is less and less likely that customers 30 or 50 years from now will actually hold coins or notes in these currencies. All our transactions might well be taking place in the virtual world of the Internet… or whatever has taking its place by then.

Opposite: new technology, such as multi-touch pads, is already revolutionizing the world of money and finance.

YOUR MONEY'S WORTH

It's your call

Americans have a saying, 'If it ain't broke, don't fix it', which can be applied to buildings, cars, laws and even economic policies. Nowadays, most people feel that the system that led to the credit crunch probably was broken, or badly in need of repair. Politicians around the world are now calling for changes

to the international economic system to prevent a recurrence of the crisis. What measures would you adopt to promote a more sensible view of credit around the world?

Globalization and microcredit

One of the most important concepts in the twenty-first century is globalization, the way in which the world seems smaller because of advances in technology, communications and transport. For people concerned about inequalities in wealth around the world, globalization is a bad thing. They believe that new high-speed and high-tech links make it easier for large companies (from the richest countries) to overwhelm the struggling industries in poorer, developing countries.

But advances do not necessarily lead to a wave of cola and fast food which washes away local businesses in the poorest countries. Instant communication has helped people in the poorest countries improve their lives. One of the most successful is called microcredit, which involves establishing banks (or branches of banks) at local – usually village – level. These banks can lend money to local farmers and those forming businesses, ie to people who did not have the chance to borrow money before.

Grameen Bank in Bangladesh was the first bank to achieve widespread success with microcredit. The bank's name comes from the local word for village, and that is where much of its business is focused. Its example has been followed by banks around the world. In 2006, the bank and its founder, Muhammad Yunus, were jointly awarded the Nobel Peace Prize.

Despite the rapid rate of change, money in some form will still 'make the world go round'. And if individuals and businesses need more funds – no matter how those funds are stored or accounted for – they will still need to borrow to make big purchases. So credit will not disappear in the future either.

In the shorter term, there may be a drop in the risky banking practices that many people believe led to the credit crunch. Big bonuses and investments tied to high-risk mortgages may be less common when the good times return: perhaps the world will have learned a lesson.

Personal account

BANKER TO THE POOR

The microcredit example set by Muhammad Yunus and the Grameen Bank has been followed by many influential people. Former US president Bill Clinton called on Yunus to help set up microcredit schemes to help the poorest people in his own state of Arkansas.

Muhammad Yunus, whose book on microcredit is called Banker to the Poor, believes that the basic justice and fairness of such schemes will ensure their success.

'Microcredit is something which is not going to disappear... because this is a need of the people. Whatever name you give it, you have to have those financial facilities coming to them because it is totally unfair... to deny half the population of the world financial services.'

Muhammad Yunus holds his Nobel Peace Prize medal and diploma at Oslo Town Hall after the award ceremony in December 2006.

Glossary

accountant   Someone who looks after the financial records of individuals or companies.

asset   Something of value owned by a person or a business.

barter   An exchange of goods without money.

bill of exchange   A document directing a third party to pay a specific amount of money to a particular person.

boom   A long period of economic confidence, when money is freely available.

budget   A prediction of how much money a family, company or country will receive and spend in a particular period.

central bank   A country's main monetary authority, which has the power to control interest rates, the supply of money and other matters related to money and credit.

commodities   Items such as precious metals which have value.

commodity money   A type of money which has value because of the commodity from which it is made, such as gold, silver or shells.

credit   The granting of a loan, which in turn creates a debt.

credit card   A system of delayed payment, which becomes a loan (to be repaid with interest) if the debt is not paid off by a certain date.

currency   A unit of exchange. The type of money (such as pound, dollar or euro) used within a country.

default   To fail to pay back (a loan, for example) on time.

developing countries   Less well-off countries, which rely on farming rather than manufacturing for their main income.

economist   A person who specializes in economics, the study of money on a large scale.

exchange rate   How much one currency is worth compared with another.

fiat money   Money that gains its value by being backed by a government.

globalization   The increasing cooperation among countries around the world, or the growing opportunities for companies to spread from one country to another.

government bond   A type of debt a government takes on, selling a document (bond) with the promise to pay back the purchase price, plus interest, later.

Great Depression   A period of economic hardship from 1929 to 1939.

inflation   The rise in prices of goods and services in an economy.

interest   A fee paid for borrowing.

International Monetary Fund (IMF)   An international organization that oversees the world financial system and offers loans to the poorest countries.

investments   Something bought in the hope that it will increase in value over time.

mature (in the case of a bond)   To reach its full value.

means testing   Assessing people's income to decide whether they qualify for benefits or other financial help.

monetary   To do with money.

mortgage   A loan to buy a house.

quantitative easing   A strategy used by the Bank of England to buy back bonds from banks and other companies. The money the banks receive can be used to increase the number of loans they make, and so help economic recovery.

representative money   Money that can be exchanged for the specific amount of gold or silver it represents.

securities   A general term describing financial investments such as bonds and shares.

share   A fraction (or share) of the value of a company, which can be bought and sold.

share price   The price paid for a single share of a company.

transaction   An agreement between a buyer and seller to exchange an asset for an agreed price.

universal benefits   Money distributed by the government to people regardless of how well off they are.

World Bank   An international financial institution that offers loans to developing countries.

Further reading

I'm Broke! The Money Handbook Liam Croke (TickTock Media, 2009)

Life Skills: Raising Money Barbara Hollander (Heinemann Library, 2008)

Money and Finance Lisa Firth (Independence Educational, 2009)

The Teenager's Guide to Money Jonathan Self (Quercus, 2007).

Websites

Bank of England Museum
www.bankofengland.co.uk/education/museum/index

BBC raw skills for everyday life
http://www.bbc.co.uk/raw/money/

Piggybank
www.piggybank.co.uk/money.php

Index